CELTIC PRAYERS
from
IONA

J. PHILIP NEWELL

PAULIST PRESS
New York / Mahwah, N.J.

Originally published in Great Britain as *Each Day and Each Night* © 1994; Wild Goose Publications/The Iona Community.

Jacket design by Cindy Dunne.

Library of Congress Cataloging-in-Publication Data

Newell, J. Philip.
    Celtic prayers from Iona / by J. Philip Newell.
        p.   cm.
    ISBN 0-8091-0488-1 (alk. paper)
    1. Prayers. 2. Iona Community. I. Title.
BV245.N494   1997
242'.802—dc21

                                                            96–48044
                                                                 CIP

Published by Paulist Press
997 Macarthur Boulevard
Mahwah, New Jersey 07430

Printed and bound in the
United States of America

LIST OF CONTENTS

Preface

This collection of morning and evening prayers has grown primarily out of my own desire for a discipline and shape in daily personal prayer. During my time as Warden of Iona Abbey, Members and Associates of the Iona Community, whose first rule is to pray and study the Scriptures each day, often expressed the need for something like a prayer book for individual use. I hope these prayers may be helpful to them and to others as well.

Many people have indicated that they would like their own prayers at home to be based on the major themes of daily prayer at the Abbey, and so I have woven the weekly themes from Iona into this six-day cycle of prayer. On Mondays, there is an emphasis on justice and peace; on Tuesdays, a concentration on prayer for healing; on Wednesdays, a focus on the goodness of Creation and care for the earth, connected with the weekly pilgrimage around the island; on Thursdays, the theme of commitment to Christ; on Fridays, a celebration of the communion of the whole Church; and on Saturdays, an emphasis on welcome and hospitality. I have assumed that on Sundays the pattern is to gather together with others to pray rather than remaining alone.

I have included in the appendix a lectionary of psalms and gospel readings which have been used in the Abbey. This is based upon the 'Consultation on Common Texts' (1978), in which many churches participated, including the Roman Catholic, the Anglican, the Presbyterian and the Methodist.

Most of the prayers in this book, their rhythms and images, are drawn from and inspired by the work of Alexander Carmichael of Edinburgh. Late in the nineteenth century, Carmichael repeatedly visited the Scottish Hebrides to transcribe the prayers and poems of the people from the sung Gaelic, and eventually published them in the *Carmina Gadelica* in 1900 (recently republished by Floris Books, Edinburgh, 1992). These 'Songs and Prayers of the Gaels' had been forged by crofters and fishermen in the often wild and harsh conditions of the Western Isles, and been passed down in the oral tradition for hundreds of years. They were recited by both Roman Catholics and Protestants, for many of the prayers had their origins in the shared stream of spirituality that flowed from the Celtic Church of Ireland and Scotland before the eleventh century.

By the nineteenth century, however, as a result of the Highland Clearances and the dispersal of community, along with the suppression of Gaelic culture and language and ways of seeing, the songs were beginning to fade in the living memory. If Carmichael had not recorded these prayers, some of the greatest riches of Scottish spirituality would, within decades, have been lost forever. The *Carmina Gadelica* has played an important part on Iona and elsewhere in the upsurge of interest in our Celtic spiritual heritage.

Carmichael's prayers lend themselves to being used in the Iona Community's weekly cycle of themes. Christ is seen as being with and for the poor; healing is regarded as a grace that releases the essential life and health of body and soul, and not in opposition to the natural process of death; and the goodness of Creation is celebrated while life is also regarded as pilgrimage. Commitment to the gospel is set within the context of an intimate relationship with a personal God; the life of heaven and the life of earth are seen as bound inextricably together; and the delights and demands of welcome and hospitality - expecting to meet Christ in the stranger's guise - are richly portrayed.

The Iona Community thoughtfully provided me with a sabbatical and I used the time in part to work on this book of prayers. I trust that they will be of help to some of us, some of the time, in our prayers of wonder and hope for the world. They are offered in the conviction that our lives are enfolded by the great mystery of God, each day and each night.

Introduction

The little island on Iona in the Western Isles of Scotland is known as one of Britain's most historic holy places. It was there in the sixth century that St. Columba established his mission from Ireland. Iona is remembered as the cradle of Christianity for much of Scotland and northern England. It is a very beautiful Hebridean island and has been described as "a thin place," in which the material realm is only thinly separated from the spiritual. The great Celtic mystic of the twentieth century, Lord MacLeod of Fuinary, who was also a Church of Scotland minister, said that the eternal is "seeping" through the physical. He was not, of course, speaking only of Iona, but of Iona as a sign of what is most deeply true of every place and every time. As the overlapping strands in Celtic artwork suggest, the life of heaven is inseparably woven into the life of earth. God is the Life within all life, the Light within all light. "Shafts of that divine light," said the fourth-century Celtic theologian, Pelagius, "penetrate the thin veil that divides heaven from earth."

The year 1997, the 1,400th anniversary of Columba's death, will be a year of increased pilgrimage to Iona as the center of the ancient Celtic Church's mission to Britain. Ironically, it will also be a year in which attention is given to Augustine of Canterbury and his Roman mission to Britain, which began around the same time as Columba's death in 597. The Celtic mission and the Roman mission represented radically different ways of seeing. The clash that resulted led to the Synod of Whitby in 664 and the tragic displacement of Celtic spirituality in Britain. Banished to the edges of British Christianity, the old Celtic Church's way of seeing was sidelined, including its emphasis on the essential goodness of creation. Celtic spirituality was now to live on, not within the four walls of the church, as it were, but outside of the formal teachings and practices of the church, primarily in the Celtic fringes of Britain.

In my book *Listening for the Heartbeat of God*, I have outlined the main characteristics of Celtic spirituality over the centuries and described how it lived on almost as a spiritual resistance movement in the Western Isles of Scotland. For hundreds of years the prayers of this spirituality were passed down in the oral tradition among the men and women of Iona and the other islands. Many of these were finally collected and transcribed in the nineteenth century by a man named Alexander Carmichael. His six-volume collection, entitled the *Carmina Gadelica (Song of the Gaels)*, conveys the distinct ways of seeing that was expressed by the people of the islands in their prayers at the rising of the sun and at its setting, for instance, or at the kindling of the fire in the morning and at its "smooring" (covering) at night. These prayers, usually chanted or sung, were not uttered in religious contexts but rather were the songs of daily life. Again and again the perspective that comes across in Celtic spirituality is that the world is the temple of God. It is there that we join our voices to the ongoing song and deepest yearnings of creation.

The prayers that Carmichael collected celebrate the essential goodness of all created life while at the same time being aware of suffering and evil. It is important not to romanticize this tradition, for it was forged in the often inhospitable conditions of the west coast of Scotland. When crops failed, there was terrible hardship, and the lives of fishermen were often lost at sea. In addition to the harshness of the elements, the people of this tradition increasingly had to face the opposition, and sometimes cruel treatment, of the religion of the land. Viewed unsympathetically by outsiders, the sun and moon prayers, for instance, were regarded by the established church not as a form of Christ mysticism but as pre-Christian pantheism. Especially from the seventeenth century onward, many ministers and headmasters forbade the use of these prayers in their parishes.

By the time Carmichael was collecting the prayers in the nineteenth century, there were accounts not only of school children being beaten for singing these songs in Gaelic but also of ministers collecting and burning the fiddles and pipes of the people to prevent them from continuing the old songs and music of the Celtic tradition. The greatest blow to their continued use were the Highland Clearances of the first half of the nineteenth century. Thousands of families were cleared from their ancestral lands and dispersed either to North America and Australia or to the streets of Glasgow. With the people torn apart from one another and from the island context in which they had sung and learned these prayers, the tradition began to falter and within a generation or two had largely been lost. If Carmichael had not made his collection from the old men and women who remained in the islands, this rich stream of prayer would soon have erased been from living memory.

Celtic Prayers from Iona is an attempt to incorporate aspects of this ancient stream into a pattern of prayer for today. It was particularly during my time as warden of Iona Abbey that I came to see that this tradition's way of seeing is a rich resource for our spirituality in the twentieth century. Initially I set out to write this book of prayers for members and associates of the Iona Community, but its British publication has proved that there is a widespread desire to recover this way of seeing in our prayer life.

Many people had indicated to me that they would like their prayers at home to be related to the major themes of worship at the abbey. The Iona Community, an ecumenical movement of men and women, lay and ordained, living and working throughout the world, regards the abbey as its island home. The weekly themes of worship on Iona reflect the community's primary concerns and commitments in different parts of Britain and beyond. On Mondays, therefore, there is an emphasis on justice and peace; on Tuesdays, a concentration on prayer for healing; on Wednesdays, a focus on the goodness of creation and care for the earth; on Thursdays, the theme of commitment to Christ; on Fridays, a celebration of the communion of the church in heaven and on earth; and on Saturdays, an emphasis on welcome and hospitality.

The more I learned of the *Carmina Gadelica* prayers, the more I believed that they could be adapted for use in the Iona Community's weekly cycle of prayer. Christ is seen, for instance, as being with and for the poor; healing is regarded as a grace that releases the essential well-being of God's life within us; creation is viewed sacramentally; Christ is portrayed as liberator of the image of God in us; the life of heaven and the life of earth are seen as bound inextricably together; and the delights and demands of welcome and hospitality—expecting to meet Christ in the stranger's guise—are accentuated. The prayers in this book, therefore, have been adapted from the words and imagery of Carmichael's collection of prayers in the oral tradition.

The rebirth of interest in things Celtic is widespread in the Western world. My hope in offering these prayers is that, in addition to reading about Celtic history, for instance, or learning more of Celtic art and spirituality, we may also have rich and simple resources for learning to pray in new ways. In praying with the Celtic saints, may our eyes be further opened to the One who is the Life within our life and all life.

J. Philip Newell
St. John's House

THE LORD'S PRAYER

Our Father in heaven
Hallowed be your name
Your kingdom come
Your will be done
     on earth as in heaven
Give us today our daily bread
Forgive us our sins
As we forgive those who sin against us
Lead us not into temptation
But deliver us from evil
For the kingdom, the power
     and the glory are yours
Now and for ever
Amen.

Monday

JUSTICE AND PEACE

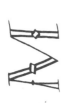

MORNING

You have searched me
and known me O God
You know when I sit down
and when I rise up

(Ps 139. 1-2)

SILENCE

Be still
and aware of God's presence
within and all around

OPENING PRAYER
AND THANKSGIVING

Thanks be to you O God

that I have risen this day
To the rising of this life itself.
May it be a day of blessing,
O God of every gift,
A day of new beginnings given.
Help me to avoid every sin
And the source of every sin to forsake
And as the mist scatters
from the crest of the hills
May each ill haze clear
from my soul O God.

FREE PRAYERS OF THANKS

THE LORD'S PRAYER

SCRIPTURE READINGS

See appendix for psalms and gospels

SILENCE

Reflect on the gospel
and remember
that God is with those
who are poor and betrayed

INTERCESSIONS

O Christ of the poor and the yearning
Kindle in my heart within
A flame of love for my neighbour,
For my foe, for my friend,
    for my kindred all.
From the humblest thing that lives
To the Name that is highest of all
Kindle in my heart within
A flame of love.

Pray for the coming day
and for justice and peace

CLOSING PRAYER

This day and this night,
  may I know O God
The deep peace
  of the running wave
The deep peace
  of the flowing air
The deep peace
  of the quiet earth
The deep peace
  of the shining stars
The deep peace
  of the Son of Peace.

EVENING

You discern my thoughts
from far away O God
You search out my path
and my lying down
And are acquainted
with all my ways

(Ps 139. 2-3)

SILENCE

Be still
and aware of God's presence
within and all around

OPENING PRAYER
AND THANKSGIVING

O Christ of the least
    and the homeless
O Christ of the lost
    and betrayed
Come close to me this night
That I may come close to you.
As you watched me with care
    at my soul's shaping
Look on me now with grace.
As you blessed me with light
    at the sun's rising
Shine on me now with love.

FREE PRAYERS OF THANKS

THE LORD'S PRAYER

SCRIPTURE READINGS

SILENCE

Reflect on the gospel
and remember
that God is with those
who are poor and betrayed

INTERCESSIONS

Peace between nations
Peace between neighbours
Peace between lovers
In love of the God of life.
Peace between man and woman
Peace between parent and child
Peace between brother and sister
The peace of Christ above all peace.
Bless O Christ my face
Let my face bless everything.
Bless O Christ my eyes
Let my eyes bless all they see.

Recall the events of the day
and pray for justice and peace

CLOSING PRAYER

I end this day
as the Son of Mary would end it.
The grace of God be on this place
And on all whom
    God has given me.
Who keeps watch
    over us this night?
Who but the Christ of love.

Tuesday

PRAYERS FOR HEALING

MORNING

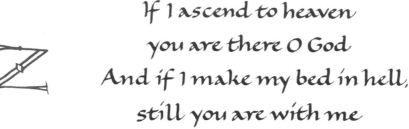

If I ascend to heaven
you are there O God
And if I make my bed in hell,
still you are with me

[Ps 139.8]

SILENCE

Be still
and aware of God's presence
within and all around

OPENING PRAYER
AND THANKSGIVING

In the beginning O God
You shaped my soul and set its weave
You formed my body
    and gave it breath.
Renew me this day
    in the image of your love.
O great God, grant me your light
O great God, grant me your grace
O great God, grant me
    your joy this day
And let me be made pure
    in the well of your health.

FREE PRAYERS OF THANKS

THE LORD'S PRAYER

SCRIPTURE READINGS

SILENCE

Reflect on the gospel
and on the Christ of the cross,
suffering in the world
with all those who are broken

INTERCESSIONS

O Christ of the road
   of the wounded
O Christ of the tears
   of the broken
In me and with me
   the needs of the world
Grant me my prayers
   of loving and hoping
Grant me my prayers
   of yearning and healing.

Pray for the coming day
  and for healing
within and among people

CLOSING PRAYER

God before me, God behind me,
God above me, God beneath me.
I on your path O God
You, O God, on my way.
In the twistings of the road
In the currents of the river
Be with me by day
Be with me by night
Be with me by day and by night.

EVENING

You are behind me
and before me O God
You lay your hand
upon me

[Ps 139.5]

SILENCE
Be still
and aware of God's presence
within and all around

OPENING PRAYER
AND THANKSGIVING

As I utter these prayers
    from my mouth O God
In my soul may I feel your presence.
The knee that is stiff
    O healer make pliant
The heart that is hard,
 make warm beneath your wing
The wound that is giving me pain,
O best of healers, make whole
And may my hopes and my fears
Find a listening place with you.

FREE PRAYERS OF THANKS

THE LORD'S PRAYER

SCRIPTURE READINGS

SILENCE

Reflect on the gospel
and on the Christ of the cross,
suffering in the world
with all those who are broken

INTERCESSIONS

O God of the stars
    and the night skies
May your light be coming through
    thick clouds this night
On me and on everyone
    coming through dark tears
On each one in need
    and in suffering.

Recall the events of the day
    and pray for healing
within and among people

CLOSING PRAYER

Christ stands before me
    and peace is in his mind.
Sleep, O sleep
    in the calm of all calm
Sleep, O sleep
    in the love of all loves
Sleep I this night
    in the God of all life.

Wednesday

THE GOODNESS OF CREATION
AND CARE FOR THE EARTH

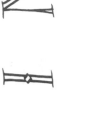

MORNING

It was you who formed
my inward parts.
You knit me together
in my mother's womb
I praise you
for I am fearfully
and wonderfully made

(Ps 139. 13–14)

SILENCE

Be still
and aware of God's presence
within and all around

OPENING PRAYER
AND THANKSGIVING

O Sun behind all suns

I give you greeting this new day.
Let all Creation praise you
Let the daylight
    and the shadows praise you
Let the fertile earth
    and the swelling sea praise you
Let the winds and the rain,
    the lightning and the thunder
    praise you
Let all that breathes,
    both male and female, praise you
And I shall praise you.
O God of all life
I give you greeting this day.

FREE PRAYERS OF THANKS

THE LORD'S PRAYER

SCRIPTURE READINGS

SILENCE

Reflect on the gospel
and on God
as the well-spring of all life

INTERCESSIONS

There is no plant in the ground
But tells of your beauty, O Christ.
There is no creature on the earth
There is no life in the sea
But proclaims your goodness.
There is no bird on the wing
There is no star in the sky
There is nothing beneath the sun
But is full of your blessing.
Lighten my understanding
of your presence all around, O Christ
Kindle my will
    to be caring for Creation.

Pray for the coming day
and for the care of the earth

CLOSING PRAYER

Bless to me O God
My soul that comes from on high.
Bless to me O God
My body that is of earth.
Bless to me O God
Each thing my eye sees
Each sound my ear hears.
Bless to me O God
Each scent that goes to my nostrils
Each taste that goes to my lips
Each ray that guides my way.

EVENING

My frame
was not hidden from you
when I was being made
in secret
intricately woven
in the depths of the earth
Your eyes beheld
my unformed substance

(Ps 139.15)

SILENCE

Be still
and aware of God's presence
within and all around

OPENING PRAYER AND THANKSGIVING

You are the love
 of each living creature O God
You are the warmth
 of the rising sun
You are the whiteness
 of the moon at night
You are the life
 of the growing earth
You are the strength
 of the waves of the sea.
Speak to me this night O God
Speak to me your truth.
Dwell with me this night O God
Dwell with me in love.

FREE PRAYERS OF THANKS

THE LORD'S PRAYER

SCRIPTURE READINGS

SILENCE

Reflect on the gospel
and on God
as the well-spring of all life

INTERCESSIONS

You are above me O God
You are beneath
You are in air
You are in earth
You are beside me
You are within.
O God of heaven,
you have made your home on earth
In the broken body of Creation..
Kindle within me
a love for you in all things.

Recall the events of the day
and pray for the care of the earth

CLOSING PRAYER

May the grace of the love
of the stars be mine
May the grace of the love
of the winds be mine
May the grace of the love
of the waters be mine
In the name of the Word
of all life.

Thursday

COMMITMENT TO CHRIST

MORNING

If I take the wings
of the morning
and settle at
the furthest limits of the sea
Even there your hand
shall lead me
and your right hand
shall hold me fast

(Ps 139. 9–10)

SILENCE
Be still
and aware of God's presence
within and all around

OPENING PRAYER
AND THANKSGIVING

O loving Christ
  who died upon the tree
Each day and each night
  I remember your love.
In my lying down
  and in my rising up
In life and in death
You are my health and my peace.
Each day and each night
  I remember your forgiveness
Bestowed on me so gently
  and generously
Each day and each night
  may I be fuller in love to you.

FREE PRAYERS OF THANKS

THE LORD'S PRAYER

SCRIPTURE READINGS

SILENCE

Reflect on the gospel
and on the One who calls us
to follow him
as the Way, the Truth and the Life

INTERCESSIONS

Life be in my speech
Truth in what I say.
The love Christ Jesus gave
Be filling every heart for me.
The love Christ Jesus gave
Be filling me for everyone.

Pray for the coming day
and to follow Christ more closely

CLOSING PRAYER

Bless to me O God
The earth beneath my feet.
Bless to me O God
The path on which I go.
Bless to me O God
The people whom I meet.
O God of all gods
bless to me my life.

If I say
"Surely the darkness
shall cover me
and the light around me
become night"
even the darkness
is not dark to you
The night is as bright
as the day, for darkness is
as light to you.

(Ps 139. 11-12)

SILENCE

Be still
and aware of God's presence
within and all around

OPENING PRAYER
AND THANKSGIVING

I am bending my knee
In the eye of the God
   who created me
In the eye of the Son
   who died for me
In the eye of the Spirit
   who moves me
In love and in desire.
For the many gifts
   you have bestowed on me
Each day and night
   each sea and land
Each weather fair
   each calm each wild
Thanks be to you O God

FREE PRAYERS OF THANKS

THE LORD'S PRAYER

SCRIPTURE READINGS

SILENCE

Reflect on the gospel
and on the One who calls us
to follow him
as the Way, the Truth and the Life

INTERCESSIONS

O God I place myself
   with those who struggle
   this night.
I am here in need
I am here in pain
I am here alone
O God help me.

Recall the events of the day
and pray for those who suffer

CLOSING PRAYER

O Christ you are a bright flame
 before me
You are a guiding star above me
You are the light and love
 I see in others' eyes.
Keep me O Christ
 in a love that is tender
Keep me O Christ
 in a love that is true
Keep me O Christ
 in a love that is strong
Tonight, tomorrow and always.

Friday

THE COMMUNION OF
HEAVEN AND EARTH

MORNING

Where can I go
from your spirit O God?

(Ps 139.7)

SILENCE
Be still
and aware of God's presence
within and all around

OPENING PRAYER
AND THANKSGIVING

I awake this morning
In the presence
of the holy angels of God.
May heaven open wide before me
Above me and around me
That I may see
the Christ of my love
And his sunlit company
In all the things of earth this day.

FREE PRAYERS OF THANKS

THE LORD'S PRAYER

SCRIPTURE READINGS

SILENCE

Reflect on the gospel
and remember that we belong
to the whole company of saints
both past and present

INTERCESSIONS

O God of life, of all life, of each life,
I offer you my prayers
In the love of Christ
In the affection of Christ
In the company of Christ.
As your own household
    desires in heaven
So may I desire on earth this day.

Pray for the coming day
    and for the Church
    throughout the world

CLOSING PRAYER

The love and affection
   of the angels be with me
The love and affection
   of the saints be with me
The love and affection
   of heaven be with me
To lead me and to cherish me
   this day.

EVENING

Where can I flee
from your presence O God?

(Ps 139.7)

SILENCE
Be still
and aware of God's presence
within and all around

OPENING PRAYER AND THANKSGIVING

My Christ, my love,
    my encircler,
Each day, each night,
Each light, each dark,
Be near me, uphold me,
My treasure, my truth.

FREE PRAYERS OF THANKS

THE LORD'S PRAYER

SCRIPTURE READINGS

SILENCE

Reflect on the gospel
and remember that we belong
to the whole company of saints
both past and present

INTERCESSIONS

Safeguard your faithful people
in the sanctuary of your love O God.
Shelter them this night
    in the shelter of the saints.
God to enfold them
God to surround them
God in their watching
God in their hoping
God in their sleeping
God in their ever-living souls.

Recall the events of the day
  and pray for the Church
throughout the world

CLOSING PRAYER

Grant to me, O Trinity of grace,
From whom all life freely flows
That no tie over-strict,
   no tie over-dear
May be between myself
   and this world.
As it was
As it is
As it shall be evermore,
With the ebb
With the flow
 O Trinity of grace.

Saturday

WELCOME
AND HOSPITALITY

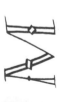

How weighty to me
are your thoughts O God
how vast is the sum of them
If I should count them
they are more than the sand
When I awake
I am still with you

(Ps 139.17-18)

SILENCE
Be still
and aware of God's presence
within and all around

OPENING PRAYER
AND THANKSGIVING

O God who brought me
   from the rest of last night
To the new light of this day
Bring me in the new light
   of this day
To the guiding light
   of the eternal.
Lead me O God
   on the journey of justice
Guide me O God
   on the pathways of peace
Renew me O God
   by the wellsprings of grace
Today, tonight and forever.

FREE PRAYERS OF THANKS

THE LORD'S PRAYER

SCRIPTURE READINGS

SILENCE

Reflect on the gospel
and remember
Jesus identifying himself
with the homeless
and the rejected

INTERCESSIONS

May those without shelter
   be under your guarding
   this day O Christ
May the wandering
   find places of welcome.
O son of the tears, of the wounds,
   of the piercings,
May your cross this day
   be shielding them.

Pray for the coming day
   and for refugees and those
without a place of welcome

CLOSING PRAYER

On my heart and on my house
The blessing of God.
In my coming and in my going
The peace of God.
In my life and in my seeking
The love of God.
At my end and new beginning
The arms of God to welcome me
and bring me home.

E V E N I N G

Search me O God
and know my heart
Test me and
know my thoughts
See if there is
any wicked way in me
and lead me
in the way everlasting

(Ps 139. 23-24)

SILENCE
Be still
and aware of God's presence
within and all around

OPENING PRAYER
AND THANKSGIVING

A shade are you in the heat O God

A shelter are you in the cold.

Eyes are you to the blind O God

A staff are you to the weak.

An island are you at sea O God

A rock are you on land.

O my soul's healer

Keep me at evening

Keep me at morning

Keep me at noon.

I am tired, astray and stumbling

Shield me from sin.

O my soul's healer

Shield me from sin.

FREE PRAYERS OF THANKS

THE LORD'S PRAYER

SCRIPTURE READINGS

SILENCE

Reflect on the gospel
and remember
Jesus identifying himself
with the homeless
and the rejected

INTERCESSIONS

Watch now O Christ
With those who are weary
   or wandering
   or weeping this night.
Guide them to a house
   of your peace
And lead me to be caring
   for their tears.

Recall the events of the day
   and pray for refugees and those
without a place of welcome

CLOSING PRAYER

I lie down this night with God
And God will lie down with me.
I lie down this night with Christ
And Christ will lie down with me.
I lie down this night with the Spirit
And the Spirit will lie down with me.
The Three of my love
    will be lying down with me.
I shall not lie down with sin
Nor shall sin or sin's shadow
    lie down with me.
I lie down this night with God
And God will lie down with me.

A WEEKDAY LECTIONARY OF PSALMS
AND GOSPEL READINGS

A lectionary is simply a list of Scripture readings. These are selected for use throughout the Church's year, which begins not on 1 January but with Advent, four weeks before Christmas.

Christmastide is followed by the seasons of Epiphany and Lent. Ash Wednesday marks the beginning of Lent and is a preparation for the season of Easter. After the weeks of Easter, the long season of Pentecost begins and finally takes us back to Advent.

The key to using a lectionary is the calendar of movable feasts. Unlike Christmas, which always falls on the same date, other major feast days, such as Easter Sunday and Pentecost, change in date from year to year. This means that in following the lectionary, it is also necessary to keep an eye on the calendar of movable feasts. There are notes throughout the lectionary to indicate when the calendar of movable feasts should be checked as a guide.

CALENDAR OF MOVABLE FEASTS

YEAR	ASH WEDNESDAY	EASTER	ASCENSION	PENTECOST	FIRST SUNDAY OF ADVENT
1997	12 February	30 March	8 May	18 May	30 November
1998	25 February	12 April	21 May	31 May	29 November
1999	17 February	4 April	13 May	23 May	28 November
2000	8 March	23 April	1 June	11 June	2 December
2001	28 February	15 April	24 May	3 June	3 December
2002	13 February	31 March	9 May	19 May	1 December
2003	5 March	20 April	29 May	8 June	30 November
2004	25 February	11 April	20 May	30 May	28 November
2005	9 February	27 March	5 May	15 May	27 November
2006	1 March	16 April	25 May	4 June	3 December

Advent 1
Week following Advent Sunday -
see calendar of movable feasts.
Mon.   Ps. 51, Matt. 8.5-13
Tues.   Ps. 57, Luke 10.21-24
Wed.   Ps. 62, Matt. 15.29-39
Thurs. Ps. 65, Matt. 7.21-27
Fri.   Ps. 67, Matt. 9.27-31
Sat.   Ps. 75, Matt. 9.35-38

Advent 2
Mon.   Ps. 77, Luke 5.17-26
Tues.   Ps. 80, Matt. 18.10-14
Wed.   Ps. 82, Matt. 11.25-30
Thurs. Ps. 84, Matt. 11.11-15
Fri.   Ps. 85, Matt. 11.16-19
Sat.   Ps. 86, Matt. 17.10-13

Advent 3
Mon.   Ps. 90, Matt. 21.23-27
Tues.   Ps. 93, Matt. 21.28-32
Wed.   Ps. 95, Luke 7.18-23
Thurs. Ps. 96, Luke 7.24-35
Fri.   Ps. 98, John 5.30-36
Sat.   Ps. 99, Matt. 1.1-17

Advent 4
If any of the days in Advent 4
fall on 24 December, go to the
Christmastide readings in the
next column.
Mon.   Ps. 100, Matt. 1.18-24
Tues.   Ps. 102, Luke 1.5-25
Wed.   Ps. 103, Luke 1.26-38
Thurs. Ps. 104.1-34, Luke 1.39-45
Fri.   Ps. 107, Luke 1.46-56
Sat.   Ps. 111, Luke 1.57-66

Christmas Eve
24 Dec.   Ps. 113, Luke 1.67-79

Christmas Day
25 Dec.   Ps. 19, John 1.1-18

Feast of St Stephen
26 Dec.   Ps. 46, John 15.20-16.4

Feast of St John
27 Dec.   Ps. 103, John 13.21-35

Holy Innocents Day
28 Dec.   Ps. 128, Matt. 18.1-10

29 Dec.   Ps. 133 and 134,
           John 12.20-33

30 Dec.   Ps. 139.1-18,
           John 12.34-50

31 Dec.   Ps. 147, Luke 21.25-36

1 Jan.   Ps. 148, Luke 2.21-40

2 Jan.   Ps. 146, John 1.19-28

3 Jan.   Ps. 150, John 1.29-34

4 Jan.   Ps. 6, John 1.35-42

5 Jan.   Ps. 113, John 1.43-51

EPIPHANY

Days at the beginning of Epiphany
Feast of Epiphany falls on 6 Jan.
6 January   Ps. 8, Matt. 2.1-12
7 January   Ps. 96, John 2.1-12 *
8 January   Ps. 13, Matt. 6.24-34 *
9 January   Ps. 98, Mark 6.45-52 *
10 January Ps. 19, Luke 4.14-30 *
11 January Ps. 23, Luke 5.12-16 *
12 January Ps. 24, John 3.22-30 *

*If this day is a Monday go to the readings in the week Epiphany 1 below.

Epiphany 1
First full week after 6 January
Mon.   Ps. 27, Mark 1.14-20
Tues.   Ps. 30, Mark 1.21-28
Wed.   Ps. 33, Mark 1.29-39
Thurs. Ps. 46, Mark 1.40-45
Fri.   Ps. 29, Mark 2.1-12
Sat.   Ps. 85, Mark 2.13-17

Epiphany 2
Mon.   Ps. 121, Mark 2.18-22
Tues.   Ps. 42, Mark 2.23-28
Wed.   Ps. 126, Mark 3.1-6
Thurs. Ps. 50, Mark 3.7-12
Fri.   Ps. 51, Mark 3.13-19
Sat.   Ps. 67, Mark 3.20-30

Epiphany 3
Mon.   Ps. 57, Mark 3.31-35
Tues.   Ps. 62, Mark 4.1-9
Wed.   Ps. 65, Mark 4.10-20
Thurs. Ps. 85, Mark 4.21-25
Fri.   Ps. 86, Mark 4.26-34
Sat.   Ps. 96, Mark 4.35-41

Epiphany 4
Mon.   Ps. 77, Mark 5.1-20
Tues.   Ps. 99, Mark 5.21-43
Wed.   Ps. 80, Mark 6.1-6
Thurs. Ps. 82, Mark 6.7-13
Fri.   Ps. 84, Mark 6.14-29
Sat.   Ps. 100, Mark 6.30-44

Epiphany 5
Mon.   Ps. 90, Mark 6.53-56
Tues.   Ps. 93, Mark 7.1-13
Wed.   Ps. 95, Mark 7.14-23
Thurs. Ps. 98, Mark 7.24-30
Fri.   Ps. 102, Mark 7.31-37
Sat.   Ps. 103, Mark 8.1-10

Check the date of Ash Wednesday in the calendar of movable feasts, and then go to the appropriate week before Lent or to the Monday before Ash Wednesday.

Third week before Lent
Mon.   Ps. 127, Mark 8.11-13
Tues.   Ps. 128, Mark 8.14-21
Wed.   Ps. 107, Mark 8.22-26
Thurs. Ps. 126, Mark 8.27-33
Fri.   Ps. 111, Mark 8.34-38
Sat.   Ps. 114, Mark 9.1-13

Second week before Lent
Mon.   Ps. 6, Mark 9.14-29
Tues.   Ps. 8, Mark 9.30-37
Wed.   Ps. 133, Mark 9.38-41
Thurs. Ps. 13, Mark 9.42-50
Fri.   Ps. 75, Mark 10.1-12
Sat.   Ps. 113, Mark 10.13-16

First week before Lent
Mon.   Ps. 20, Mark 10.17-27
Tues.   Ps. 23, Mark 10.28-31
Wed.   Ps. 116, Mark 10.32-45
Thurs. Ps. 118, Mark 10.46-52
Fri.   Ps. 139.1-18, Mark 11.11-26
Sat.   Ps. 24, Mark 11.27-33

LENT

Week in which Lent begins
Mon.   Ps. 57, Mark 12.1-12
Tues.   Ps. 103, Mark 12.13-17
Ash Wednesday
Wed.   Ps. 102, Matt. 6.1-21
Thurs. Ps. 42, Luke 9.18-27
Fri.   Ps. 43, Matt. 9.14-17
Sat.   Ps. 46, Luke 5.27-32

Lent 1
Mon.   Ps. 51, Matt. 25.31-46
Tues.   Ps. 50, Luke 11.1-13
Wed.   Ps. 139.1-18, Luke 11.29-32
Thurs. Ps. 62, Matt. 7.7-12
Fri.   Ps. 65, Matt. 5.21-26
Sat.   Ps. 67, Matt. 5.43-48

Lent 2
Mon.   Ps. 19, Luke 6.37-42
Tues.   Ps. 27, Matt. 23.1-12
Wed.   Ps. 75, Matt. 20.17-28
Thurs. Ps. 77, Luke 16.19-31
Fri.   Ps. 30, Matt. 21.33-46
Sat.   Ps. 80, Luke 15.11-32

Lent 3
Mon.   Ps. 82, Luke 4.16-30
Tues.   Ps. 84, Matt. 18.21-35
Wed.   Ps. 86, Matt. 5.17-20

Thurs. Ps. 90, Luke 11.14-23
Fri.   Ps. 93, Mark 12.28-34
Sat.   Ps. 95, Luke 18.9-14

Lent 4
Mon.   Ps. 99, John 4.43-54
Tues.   Ps. 103, John 5.1-18
Wed.   Ps. 104, John 5.19-29
Thurs. Ps. 107, John 5.30-47
Fri.   Ps. 111, John 7.1-24
Sat.   Ps. 113, John 7.25-30

Lent 5
Mon.   Ps. 114, John 8.1-11
Tues.   Ps. 116, John 8.21-30
Wed.   Ps. 118, John 8.31-47
Thurs. Ps. 121, John 8.48-59
Fri.   Ps. 123, John 10.22-42
Sat.   Ps. 43, John 11.45-57

Holy Week
Mon.   Ps. 25, John 12.1-11
Tues.   Ps. 27, John 12.37-50
Wed.   Ps. 22, John 13.21-35
Thurs. Ps. 42, John 13.1-15
Fri.   Ps. 130, John 18.1-19.37
Sat.   Ps. 116, John 19.38-42

EASTER

Easter Week
Easter Day
Sun.   Ps. 113, John 20.1-18
Mon.   Ps. 122, Matt. 28.11-15
Tues.   Ps. 124, John 20.19-29
Wed.   Ps. 127, Luke 24.13-35
Thurs. Ps. 133, 134, Luke 24.36-49
Fri.   Ps. 138, John 21.1-14
Sat.   Ps. 139.1-18, Mark 16.9-18

Easter 1

Mon.	Ps. 146, John 3.1-8
Tues.	Ps. 147, John 3.9-13
Wed.	Ps. 148, John 3.14-21
Thurs.	Ps. 150, John 3.31-36
Fri.	Ps. 46, John 6.1-15
Sat.	Ps. 29, John 6.16-21

Easter 2

Mon.	Ps. 8, John 6.22-29
Tues.	Ps. 13, John 6.30-35
Wed.	Ps. 16, John 6.35-40
Thurs.	Ps. 19, John 6.44-51
Fri.	Ps. 20, John 6.53-59
Sat.	Ps. 23, John 6.60-69

Easter 3

Mon.	Ps. 24, John 10.1-8
Tues.	Ps. 25, John 10.9-18
Wed.	Ps. 27, John 12.44-50
Thurs.	Ps. 29, John 13.16-20
Fri.	Ps. 30, John 14.1-6
Sat.	Ps. 33, John 14.7-14

Easter 4

Mon.	Ps. 42, John 14.21-26
Tues.	Ps. 43, John 14.27-31
Wed.	Ps. 46, John 15.1-8
Thurs.	Ps. 50, John 15.9-11
Fri.	Ps. 51, John 15.12-17
Sat.	Ps. 57, John 15.18-21

Easter 5

Mon.	Ps. 62, John 15.26-16.4
Tues.	Ps. 65, John 16.5-11
Wed.	Ps. 67, John 16.12-15
Ascension Day	
Thurs.	Ps. 96, Luke 24.44-53
Fri.	Ps. 75, John 16.20-23
Sat.	Ps. 77, John 16.24-28

Easter 6

Mon.	Ps. 121, John 16.29-33
Tues.	Ps. 126, John 17.1-11
Wed.	Ps. 138, John 17.12-19
Thurs.	Ps. 150, John 17.20-26
Fri.	Ps. 80, John 21.15-19
Sat.	Ps. 104.1-34, John 21.20-25

PENTECOST

The season of Pentecost can begin as early as 10 May and as late as 13 June. See the date of Pentecost in the calendar of movable feasts and go to the appropriate week.

Week beginning Sun. 8-14 May

Mon.	Ps. 82, Matt. 5.1-12
Tues.	Ps. 84, Matt. 5.13-16
Wed.	Ps. 85, Matt. 5.17-20
Thurs.	Ps. 86, Matt. 5.21-26
Fri.	Ps. 90, Matt. 5.27-32
Sat.	Ps. 93, Matt. 5.33-37

Week beginning 15-21 May

Mon.	Ps. 95, Matt. 5.38-42
Tues.	Ps. 96, Matt. 5.43-48
Wed.	Ps. 98, Matt. 6.1-6
Thurs.	Ps. 99, Matt. 6.7-15
Fri.	Ps. 100, Matt. 6.16-18
Sat.	Ps. 102, Matt. 6.19-23

Week beginning 22-28 May

Mon.	Ps. 103, Matt. 6.24-34
Tues.	Ps. 104.1-34, Matt. 7.1-6
Wed.	Ps. 107, Matt. 7.7-11
Thurs.	Ps. 111, Matt. 7.12-14
Fri.	Ps. 113, Matt. 7.15-20
Sat.	Ps. 114, Matt. 7.21-29

Week beginning 29 May - 4 June

Mon.	Ps. 116, Matt. 8.1-4
Tues.	Ps. 118, Matt. 8.5-13
Wed.	Ps. 121, Matt. 8.14-17
Thurs.	Ps. 122, Matt. 8.18-22
Fri.	Ps. 123, Matt. 8.23-27
Sat.	Ps. 124, Matt. 8.28-34

Week beginning 5-11 June

Mon.	Ps. 126, Matt. 9.1-8
Tues.	Ps. 127, Matt. 9.9-13
Wed.	Ps. 128, Matt. 9.14-17
Thurs.	Ps. 130, Matt. 9.18-26
Fri.	Ps. 133, 134, Matt. 9.27-31
Sat.	Ps. 138, Matt. 9.32-38

Week beginning 12-18 June

Mon.	Ps. 139.1-18, Matt. 10.1-7
Tues.	Ps. 146, Matt. 10.7-15
Wed.	Ps. 147, Matt. 10.16-23
Thurs.	Ps. 148, Matt. 10.24-33
Fri.	Ps. 150, Matt. 10.34-39
Sat.	Ps. 6, Matt. 10.40-42

Week beginning 19-25 June

Mon.	Ps. 8, Matt. 11.1-6
Tues.	Ps. 13, Matt. 11.7-15
Wed.	Ps. 16, Matt. 11.16-19
Thurs.	Ps. 19, Matt. 11.20-24
Fri.	Ps. 20, Matt. 11.25-27
Sat.	Ps. 22, Matt. 11.28-30

Week beginning 26 June - 2 July

Mon.	Ps. 23, Matt. 12.1-8
Tues.	Ps. 24, Matt. 12.14-21
Wed.	Ps. 25, Matt. 12.33-37
Thurs.	Ps. 27, Matt. 12.38-42
Fri.	Ps. 29, Matt. 12.43-45
Sat.	Ps. 30, Matt. 12.46-50

Week beginning 3-9 July

Mon.	Ps. 33, Matt. 13.1-9
Tues.	Ps. 42, Matt. 13.10-17
Wed.	Ps. 43, Matt. 13.18-23
Thurs.	Ps. 46, Matt. 13.24-30
Fri.	Ps. 50, Matt. 13.31-35
Sat.	Ps. 51, Matt. 13.36-43

Week beginning 10-16 July

Mon.	Ps. 57, Matt. 13.44-46
Tues.	Ps. 62, Matt. 13.47-52
Wed.	Ps. 65, Matt. 13.53-58
Thurs.	Ps. 67, Matt. 14.1-12
Fri.	Ps. 75, Matt. 14.13-21
Sat.	Ps. 77, Matt. 14.22-36

Week beginning 17-23 July

Mon.	Ps. 80, Matt. 15.1-9
Tues.	Ps. 82, Matt. 15.10-20
Wed.	Ps. 84, Matt. 15.21-28
Thurs.	Ps. 85, Matt. 15.29-31
Fri.	Ps. 86, Matt. 15.32-39
Sat.	Ps. 90, Matt. 16.1-4

Week beginning 24-30 July

Mon.	Ps. 93, Matt. 16.5-12
Tues.	Ps. 95, Matt. 16.13-23
Wed.	Ps. 96, Matt. 16.24-28
Thurs.	Ps. 98, Matt. 17.1-8
Fri.	Ps. 99, Matt. 17.14-21
Sat.	Ps. 100, Matt. 17.22-27

Week beginning 31 July - 6 August

Mon.	Ps. 102, Matt. 18.1-14
Tues.	Ps. 103, Matt. 18.15-20
Wed.	Ps. 104.1-34, Matt. 18.21-35
Thurs.	Ps. 107, Matt. 19.1-12
Fri.	Ps. 111, Matt. 19.13-15
Sat.	Ps. 113, Matt. 19.16-22

Week beginning 7-13 August
Mon.   Ps. 114, Matt. 19.23-30
Tues.   Ps. 116, Matt. 20.1-16
Wed.   Ps. 118, Matt. 22.1-14
Thurs. Ps. 121, Matt. 22.34-40
Fri.   Ps. 122, Matt. 23.1-12
Sat.   Ps. 123, Matt. 23.13-22

Week beginning 14-20 August
Mon.   Ps. 124, Matt. 23.23-26
Tues.   Ps. 126, Matt. 23.27-32
Wed.   Ps. 127, Matt. 24.42-51
Thurs. Ps. 128, Matt. 25.1-13
Fri.   Ps. 130, Matt. 25.14-30
Sat.   Ps. 133, 134, Matt. 25.31-40

Week beginning 21-27 August
Mon.   Ps. 138, Luke 4.16-30
Tues.   Ps. 139.1-18, Luke 4.31-37
Wed.   Ps. 146, Luke 4.38-41
Thurs. Ps. 147, Luke 4.42-44
Fri.   Ps. 148, Luke 5.1-11
Sat.   Ps. 150, Luke 5.12-16

Week beginning 28 Aug. - 3 Sept.
Mon.   Ps. 6, Luke 5.17-26
Tues.   Ps. 8, Luke 5.27-32
Wed.   Ps. 13, Luke 5.33-39
Thurs. Ps. 16, Luke 6.1-5
Fri.   Ps. 19, Luke 6.6-11
Sat.   Ps. 20, Luke 6.12-19

Week beginning 4-10 September
Mon.   Ps. 22, Luke 6.20-26
Tues.   Ps. 23, Luke 6.27-31
Wed.   Ps. 24, Luke 6.32-36
Thurs. Ps. 25, Luke 6.37-38
Fri.   Ps. 27, Luke 6.39-42
Sat.   Ps. 29, Luke 6.43-49

Week beginning 11-17 September
Mon.   Ps. 30, Luke 7.1-10
Tues.   Ps. 33, Luke 7.11-17
Wed.   Ps. 42, Luke 7.31-35
Thurs. Ps. 43, Luke 7.36-50
Fri.   Ps. 46, Luke 8.1-3
Sat.   Ps. 50, Luke 8.4-15

Week beginning 18-24 September
Mon.   Ps. 51, Luke 8.16-18
Tues.   Ps. 57, Luke 8.19-21
Wed.   Ps. 62, Luke 9.1-6
Thurs. Ps. 65, Luke 9.7-9
Fri.   Ps. 67, Luke 9.18-22
Sat.   Ps. 75, Luke 9.44-45

Week beginning 25 Sept. - 1 Oct.
Mon.   Ps. 80, Luke 9.46-50
Tues.   Ps. 82, Luke 9.51-56
Wed.   Ps. 84, Luke 9.57-62
Thurs. Ps. 85, Luke 10.1-12
Fri.   Ps. 86, Luke 10.13-16
Sat.   Ps. 90, Luke 10.17-24

Week beginning 2-8 October
Mon.   Ps. 93, Luke 10.25-37
Tues.   Ps. 95, Luke 10.38-42
Wed.   Ps. 96, Luke 11.1-4
Thurs. Ps. 98, Luke 11.5-13
Fri.   Ps. 99, Luke 11.14-26
Sat.   Ps. 100, Luke 11.27-28

Week beginning 9-15 October
Mon.   Ps. 102, Luke 11.29-32
Tues.   Ps. 103, Luke 11.37-41
Wed.   Ps. 104.1-34, Luke 11.42-46
Thurs. Ps. 107, Luke 11.47-54
Fri.   Ps. 111, Luke 12.1-7
Sat.   Ps. 113, Luke 12.8-12

Week beginning 16-22 October

Mon.   Ps. 114, Luke 12.13-21
Tues. Ps. 116, Luke 12.35-40
Wed.   Ps. 118, Luke 12.41-48
Thurs. Ps. 121, Luke 12.49-53
Fri.   Ps. 122, Luke 12.54-59
Sat.   Ps. 123, Luke 13.1-9

Week beginning 23-29 October

Mon.   Ps. 124, Luke 13.10-17
Tues. Ps. 126, Luke 13.18-21
Wed.   Ps. 127, Luke 13.22-30
Thurs. Ps. 128, Luke 13.31-35
Fri.   Ps. 130, Luke 14.1-6
Sat.   Ps. 133, 134, Luke 14.7-11

Week beginning 30 Oct. - 5 Nov.

Mon.   Ps. 138, Luke 14.12-14
Tues. Ps. 139.1-18, Luke 14.15-24
Wed.   Ps. 146, Luke 14.25-33
Thurs. Ps. 147, Luke 15.1-10
Fri.   Ps. 148, Luke 16.1-8
Sat.   Ps. 150, Luke 16.9-15

Week beginning 6-12 November

Mon.   Ps. 6, Luke 17.1-6
Tues. Ps. 8, Luke 17.7-10
Wed.   Ps. 13, Luke 17.11-19
Thurs. Ps. 16, Luke 17.20-25
Fri.   Ps. 19, Luke 17.26-37
Sat.   Ps. 20, Luke 18.1-8

Week beginning 13-19 November

Mon.   Ps. 22, Luke 18.35-43
Tues. Ps. 23, Luke 19.1-10
Wed.   Ps. 24, Luke 19.11-28
Thurs. Ps. 25, Luke 19.41-44
Fri.   Ps. 27, Luke 19.45-48
Sat.   Ps. 29, Luke 20.27-40

Week Before Advent

Mon.   Ps. 30, Luke 21.1-4
Tues. Ps. 33, Luke 21.5-11
Wed.   Ps. 42, Luke 21.12-19
Thurs. Ps. 43, Luke 21.20-28
Fri.   Ps. 46, Luke 21.29-33
Sat.   Ps. 50, Luke 21.34-38

THE IONA COMMUNITY

The Iona Community owes its very existence to the continuing conviction that Christian community is not an abstract utopian vision, but is to be discovered, pursued and celebrated at street level and in the very midst of life.

The roots of the Iona Community extend back to 1938, to the late George MacLeod's vision to rebuild the medieval abbey which lay on the site of Saint Columba's sixth-century monastic settlement on Iona, on the West Coast of Scotland. Iona was renowned as an important centre of Celtic Christianity and the Benedictines began building the Abbey in the thirteenth century. It flourished and grew until the Reformation when it fell into disrepair. In 1938, George MacLeod, who as a minister in industrial Glasgow had felt most keenly the huge gulf between the Church and the working people of that time, led skilled craftsmen and ministers to work together to rebuild the abbey and forge the beginnings of a Christian community based on the idea that faith finds reality in the workings of everyday life.

Today, the Iona Community is an ecumenical organisation. It is part of the Church of Scotland but it is open to people of any denomination. Members are men and women, lay and ordained, from Scotland, England and other parts of the world, whose commitment to the Community is expressed in their ordinary places of life and work, in prayer, economic sharing, meeting together and working towards justice and peace. More than a thousand Associates support the Community's work through daily prayer and financial contribution, while Friends of the Community also offer financial support.

At the Abbey and the MacLeod Centre on Iona, and at Camas on Mull, a small resident group of staff and volunteers welcome guests to share in a common life of work, worship and recreation. The Community's leader, administrative staff, Wild Goose Resource Group, youth development worker and publishing section are based in Govan, Glasgow, where George MacLeod originally had his ministry, while it also funds a peace worker based in Perthshire. Through all these different strands the vision of Christian community develops and evolves and, as one of the community's prayers puts it, new ways are sought 'to touch the hearts of all'.

For more information contact
The Iona Community, Pearce Institute, Govan, Glasgow G51 3UU
Phone 041 445 4561 Fax. 041 445 4295